A Pig's
Little Instruction Book

A Pig's
Little Instruction Book

David Brawn

Thorsons
An Imprint of HarperCollins*Publishers*

Thorsons
An Imprint of HarperCollins*Publishers*
77–85 Fulham Palace Road
Hammersmith, London W6 8JB

Published by Thorsons 1996
1 3 5 7 9 10 8 6 4 2

David Brawn asserts the moral right to
be identified as the author of this work

Illustrations by David Hearn

A catalogue record for this book
is available from the British Library

ISBN 0 7225 3339 X

Printed in Great Britain by
Caledonian International Book Manufacturing Ltd, Glasgow

To Richard
For sacrificing bacon sandwiches
for the love of a woman

And to Karin
For not giving in

Introduction

Pigs are cute. Apparently.

People are crazy about them – fluffy or sculptured, they have become the collectables of the '90s. (But if you are reading this, you probably know that by now.) Indeed, since writing this book a pig has even become a major film star! However, the pig's legacy actually goes back a very long way.

Pigs populate many of our folk tales and their antics and attributes have given birth to a whole litter of phrases into our language. Furthermore, there has always been the popular image of the pig as a friendly soul who needs looking after – though pig farmers, who have to deal with the pig as flesh and blood rather than some surrogate teddy bear, would argue that little piggies are rather more robust than they are given credit for and that people have only ever really been interested in safeguarding their freezer stocks!

A Pig's Little Instruction Book draws on all these strands, so you will find big bad wolves, male chauvinists, pig farmers and pork butchers all drawn together like a string of sausages. I just hope the pearls shine out from what one might choose otherwise to describe as something of a pig's breakfast!

I also hope that, like me, your exposure to the world of the pig will enhance your appreciation of his contribution to our culture (as well as our food chain). They *can* be cute, although real pigs do tend to smell and some of the big ones have a reputation for being awkward and vicious, which makes 'cute' rather difficult to pull off. In compiling this Instruction Book I have grown rather fond of them, although it has become clear that out of the context of food production the real pig sadly no longer exists.

Thanks, Piggy – we owe you!

Never trust a veterinary who says you can be cured

 When building your house, use architect-approved materials

 Don't be the one who goes 'Wee Wee Wee' all the way home

Spot the novice pig farmer by his use of excessive jargon – swine husbandry indeed!

 Don't fret – a Landrace is the indigenous breed, not an event calling for over-exertion

Watch where you're treading

 Consider sleeping to be one of life's therapies

 If someone calls you a tremendous boar, be sure of their intentions

Imitate a film star – stutter

 If you're investigating a crime, a young sow will have gilt written all over her

 As a piglet, avoid others' germs – always know which teat is yours

Tell the politicians, before there's a Eurosausage, they'll have to find a Europig

 Wonder if you were once a human baby, like the one in *Alice in Wonderland*

 Don't lower yourself to jig-dancing

Cause a stir – go flying

 If you want to tread the boards,
don't be a ham

 Live in fear of the sausage machine

Get a job that pays well – be a truffle hunter

 Seek out a pig who actually says 'oink'

 Don't make a pig's breakfast out of anything (unless it's the first meal of the day)

As an insult, 'Pig-Dog' only sounds effective in its original German

 Boycott *Peanuts* for its unsavoury 'Pigpen' character

 Don't aspire to the heights of Society and then fall in love with a frog

Only allow the nickname 'Piggy-wig' if you have a ring through the end of your nose

 The farmer's favourite, 'A happy pig makes happy bacon,' is reassuring but flawed – it's a dead pig who makes bacon!

Challenge the right of an overgrown pincushion to bear the noble name of guinea *pig*

 Decide whether being genetically closer to man than other mammals is something to be proud of

Get your revenge – dung in a rival's water trough

 Don't just lie in the sun – *bask* in it

 Know that, properly used, 'pig's ear' is slang for beer, not a complete mess

Pity anybody – literary megastar or no – with the name Bland

 Buy a crackling good adventure story to read on your holiday

Don't be a sucker – avoid the medieval banquet

 Read the seafaring derring-do of Captain Pugwash and his ship, the *Black Pig*

Find a patch of clover, sit down, and wonder what the big deal is

 Invest – buy a piggy bank

 Don't swear – never use words like 'streaky' in polite company

If you must choose an overweight bear
as your best friend, at least find one with an
ounce of brain

 Make a fashion statement – pigtails are cute,
pink and curly, not hairy sprouting bunches
that come in pairs!

Don't be ashamed of being a male chauvinist – after all, you invented it

 Who wants a silk purse anyway?

 Don't let your libido get the better of your appetite

Don't be pig sick – envy is a deadly sin, after all

 Pour scorn on those who refer to snoring as 'driving pigs'

Refuse to let some oink call you 'Babe' as a chat-up line

 Nurture the runt of the litter to good health

Don't be mistaken into thinking that those who refer to the constabulary as 'pigs' intend it to be complimentary

 Don't fret – pig-ignorance is pig-bliss

Remember, an apple in the tree is worth two in the mouth

 Don't peek through the blindfold when playing 'squeak-piggy-squeak'

Live up to tradition – do not be stopped in a poke by a bow-legged man

 Buy a bilingual *olde worlde* dictionary to discover what a 'poke' is

 Only offer a piggy-back to one who is lighter than you

Tell your husband that these days a pig-wife wants more out of life than just selling crockery

 Offer to model for 'Piggy in my Pocket'

Don't trust anyone with hair on the end of their chinny-chin-chin

 Demand respect – make them call you *Mister* Pig

Roast beef is not a good diet for a healthy porcine constitution (you might catch mad cow disease!)

 Don't get prickly when you're homesick – you might be accused of being a pork-u-pine!

Small is beautiful – that's why small things are called pigmies

 Never feel guilty about taking a long afternoon nap (and a beforenoon one, too)

 Don't tell porky pies

Watch your weight (Don't do anything about it, just watch!)

 Remind the other animals that, in *Animal Farm*, it was the pigs who took charge

Tell people that *they'd* be ham-fisted with trotters to cope with

 Do not hide your disgust at the thought of pork scratchings

Forage for apples, but be less enthusiastic about apple sauce

 In business, never mind the peaks – anticipate the troughs!

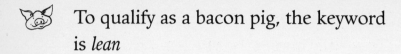 To qualify as a bacon pig, the keyword is *lean*

Treat yourself – pig out in someone's kitchen garden

Share things – don't hog them

Take human beings with a pinch of salt – they do the same with pigs!

 Be partial to a piece of fruit

 Be especially partial to a bucket of fruit

Don't mix with the sheep – they're such woolly thinkers!

 Don't contemplate pigswill for too long – just tuck in!

Pray that one day someone might buy you a Vapona for your birthday

 Keep an illicit copy of *Pigbreeders' Monthly* hidden under your bed

See that film tragedy *A Private Function*

 Count your blessings – there's always someone worse off than you (like the little piggy who had none)

Don't let a bear with poor dress sense call you 'Podgy' – unless that *is* your real name

 Take pride in your surroundings – don't leave your pigsty like a bedroom

 Go under the assumed name of Sue E.

Don't take arrogance from the cattle –
there's nothing they can do in a china
shop that you couldn't

 Don't turn your nose up at potato
peelings – most of the goodness *is*
in the skins

Take part in DIY – leave bottom prints in drying paint

 Explain to your optician you can't help having piggy eyes

 Know your own strength – and put it to good disruptive use!

Campaign for more homes for retired pigs – if donkeys can have sanctuaries, why not pigs?

 Give up acorns for Lent (it's easier – they're not in season then...)

The disadvantage of coming from a large litter is having to buy all those birthday cards

 The advantage is it's easier to remember everyone's birthday

For a competitive sport, take up mud wrestling

 Be gallant – compliment a lady pig if you notice she's put on weight

Show restraint – make your elevenses last until five past

 Be suspicious of the 'masseur' who wants to rub you down with cooking oil

Have your nose pierced professionally –
not with an icecube and a needle

 Spare a thought for the turkey on
Christmas Day (not to mention
Mr Sausagemeat)

If you're a black pig, say so – don't let the pinkies call you 'coloured'

 Never put off until tomorrow what you can eat today

Be brave, even if you happen to be only a Very Small Animal

 Never accuse another of being as thick as *that*

Avoid any opportunity to go swimming –
it's too much like having a bath

 Don't resort to cosmetic surgery –
particularly liposuction (there'd
be nothing left!)

Consider the linguistics behind sow (*n*) and sow (*v*) – but don't boar people with it

 Demand equal treatment with cows – like 'pigskin', insist on referring to leather as 'cowskin'

Wish that someone would write a song about your mother, like they did about Little Pig Robinson's

 Always eat to capacity – and still have room for some after dinner mince

Acquaint yourself with the Classics –
read *Pig-malion*

 When someone mentions 'The Pig Apple',
they must be talking about New Pork

 If you're given a straw hat, don't wear
it – eat it!

Don't refer to Mrs Pig as 'an old sow-and-sow'

 Tell complicated stories and call them curly tales

 After the 'all-day breakfast', campaign for the 'all-night midnight feast'

Look on the bright side – when did you last hear of a headless *pig* running round the farmyard?

 Play up in the showring

Ponder on why the Large White breed isn't called the Large Pink

 Beware the food scientist who has plans to cross you with a dachshund

Read the *Hip and Sty Diet* – and wonder what *is* a waistline anyway?

 Girls, beware the boar who offers you a serving crate – it's a sex aid, not a food parcel!

If you live on a farm, establish whether your pig farmer is a fattener or a breeder – it could save embarrassment later on

 Aspire to building your dream home in the middle of an orchard

Don't throw the piglet out with the trough water

 In the event of gynaecological problems, avoid seeing the semi-retired vet who just likes to keep his hand in!

Don't let anyone tell you that pink is not your colour

 Forget the New Age – don't talk to anything that can be eaten as a vegetable

Be modest – don't call yourself 'Oscar'

 Recite positive affirmations, like, 'Every day, in every way, I'm getting fatter and fatter'

Support the Royals – follow the exploits of the Duke of Pork

 Don't get caught by the short and curly

 Don't let children assume that saddlebacks give rides

To 'throw a leg across a pigskin' means to get into a saddle – it is not a legover situation for pigs!

 Face facts – belly pork might sound unattractive, but tummy pork would be plain silly

Don't let them call you Baldrick just because you have a fondness for turnips

 Never DIY if you can get someone to DI for you

 Rock'n'roll to the strains of 'Piggy Sue'

Consider – if ham were given its rightful name of 'buttock', would people still ask for it in their sandwiches?

 Point out to paganists who give the goat such a hard time that you too have cloven hooves

Tell animal rights activists they've got it all wrong – would they worry about numbers of people in a truck if farmers still castrated *them* without anaesthetic?

 Be outraged at the misrepresentation of 'toad in the hole'

Be careful not to trap your pinkies in the barn door

 Frighten other porklings with tales of the bacon slicer

 If you're feeling frisky, don't give the game away by frothing at the mouth

Be positive – if you feel in the pink,
tell the world!

 Don't ignore any pearls you might
find lying around

Swine fever cannot be cured by two
paracetamol and an early night

 Take heart – 'hammy' actors are probably
being compared to a small rodent

Marvel at the foresight of whoever named America's first supermarket chain *Piggly-Wiggly's*

 Don't listen to people who say pigs can't fly – they have no imagination!

When the butcher calls for your best friend, you can bet you won't feel as cut up about it as she does

 As a protest, learn to recite the alphabet without the letters B, L or T

Do someone a good turn – poo on their rosebushes

 Don't worry about your partner ever being unable to bring home the bacon

 If a foreign pig comes to stay, simply grunt more loudly at him to be understood

Safeguard your house – persuade Mr Wolf
to stick to dressing up as old ladies and
chasing little girls in red overcoats

 If you go hunting for Heffalumps,
take a friend with you

Don't be too picky about your food,
but resist spam fritters on grounds of good
taste

 Have an aversion to the jelly in a pork
pie (and the pork)

Take solace from the fact that 'to stare like a stuck pig' is no longer in common usage*

 If cleanliness is next to Godliness, become an atheist

*Until resurrected by *A Pig's Little Instruction Book*

Drink at The Blue Boar or The Pig
and Whistle

 Have a favourite word, like 'appetite'

 Mind your snout on thorn bushes

Don't take steroids, especially if you're competing in something athletic (as if!)

 Dream of running away from home and joining the circus

 Plead with the circus owner to let you perform *sans* tutu

If you're snacking, always favour cheese and onion as opposed to smokey bacon

 It is a myth that they all eat black pudding in Porkshire

 Demand a Pigges Week annual festival – like Cowes Week, of course

Don't buy 'fast food' – just eat normal food very quickly

 Eat your greens – especially someone's prize topiary

 When you get behind the wheel, don't automatically act like a road hog

Show *some* taste – if your house is made of straw or sticks, don't try to disguise it with stone cladding

 Don't be fooled by a pheromone spray

Don't become obsessed about cellulite

 Write your own sequels – what *did* happen to Piglet when he finally grew up to be Pig? Was Pooh disgruntled?

Dismiss any feelings of envy – the other pig's grass is *not* always squelchier

 See the funny side of a garden gnome – but despise garden ornaments in the shape of a pig!

Unless you're Vietnamese, there's no excuse for a pot belly

 If you make a commitment, go the whole hog

Don't get caught with your snout in the trough

 Be clear about your ailment if you have a sty on your eyelid

Even when wallowing in mud, assert that pigs are naturally very clean animals

 Shudder at the thought of pork pie, hamburgers, spam and brawn

Pity the farmer who thinks that size *is* important

 Embrace good fortune every 12 years – in the Year of the Pig

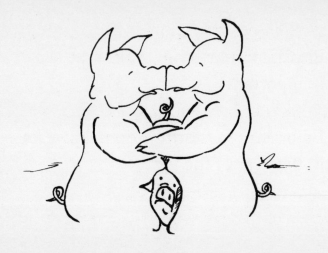

Avoid nursery rhymes – they reinforce
unflattering stereotypes

 Don't cut off your nose to spite your face –
who'd want a pig with 'snout taken out'?

 Don't hang around with couples –
nobody likes being piggy-in-the-middle

Calling your piglets 'Sage' and 'Onion' would be cruel

 If you tell a joke, make sure it's a real porker

Re-evaluate those teenage heart-throbs –
play Pinky and Perky records at half speed

 Do not treat a birdbath as a source
of refreshment

Enjoy a good scratch on a gatepost

 Be the first one to the morning porridge

 If you're in favour, give it the trotters up

Enjoy a good film, like *Live and Let Sty*, *Octopiggy* and *Goldtrotter*

 Be enigmatic – don't disclose your age to the pork butcher

Don't enter a sheepdog trial unless you think you have a good chance of winning

 Don't lie all day in direct sunlight without your suncream on

 Be PC (Pig Conscious)

Wonder if truly pink pigs are a pigment of the imagination

 Don't overdo it – watch the grass grow, *then* trample on it

Don't eat out unless you can guarantee you'll have a swill time

 Be honest and faithful to your sow – not a pigamist

Think – if the High Pig had intended boneless pork, you'd be a big pink slug

 Shrug off the 'pigs are cute' reputation – fart at a party of schoolchildren

Take stock before making any rasher decisions

 Don't take pig iron for anaemia

 Prolong your life – go on a diet

Talk in clichés 'til the pigs come home

 Take a close interest in passing wildlife – but not the hedgehog or the skunk

 Root for nuts, and be nuts about roots

If you must have a tattoo, go for something more original than *DANISH*

 Marvel at the literary prowess of whoever wrote, 'To market, to market, to buy a fat pig...'!

Don't allow the opening of a local pork kebab house without a skewered's inquiry

 Don't let a speak-your-weight machine upset you

Spare a moment's silence when the knacker calls

 If you write a book, forego the launch party in favour of a *lunch* party

Take pride in your appearance,
and don't let anyone call you 'baldy'

 Be philosophical – ending up in a German
sausage is the Wurst that can happen to you

By the same author…

A Teddy Bear's Little Instruction Book

Never serve your porridge then go out for a walk

Don't wear your duffle coat in the house

If you're made of mohair, ponder on the nature of a mo

Don't be part exchanged for a computer game

Be brave – sleep with the light off

Don't become a projectile in domestic disputes

Follow fashion – don't be the bear behind

A Dog's Little Instruction Book

Don't drink from a bowl with CAT on it

Keep your tail down when it's windy

Make friends with the local butcher

Never be seen in tartan

Don't eat slug pellets (or slugs)

Chase frisbees but not boomerangs

When you get old, learn some new tricks

A Baby's Little Instruction Book

Never be seen in a frilly sunhat

Fill your nappy immediately it's been changed

Sneeze with your mouth full

Refuse to eat your dinner, yet have room for dessert

Be an angel at the childminder's and a monster at home

Stamp your feet when you can't get your own way

Disfigure your teddy bear with too much love